Jacob

THE TROJAN HORSE

THE FALL OF TROY

A GREEK LEGEND

STORY BY
JUSTINE & RON FONTES

PENCILS BY
GORDON PURCELL

INKS BY
BARBARA SCHULZ

ADAPTED FROM VIRGIL'S *AENEID*
AND *THE WAR AT TROY*
BY QUINTUS OF SMYRNA

MOUNT
OLYMPUS

A E G E A N

GREECE

ITHACA

THEBES

MYCENAE

ATHENS

SPARTA

N

THE TROJAN HORSE

THE FALL OF TROY

A
GREEK
LEGEND

TENEDOS   •TROY

SEA

TURKEY

GRAPHIC UNIVERSE™•MINNEAPOLIS

Ancient legends of a war between the greek city states and Troy that may have taken place around 1200 b.c. were gathered into great epic poems by writers of later times. The Greek poet Homer wrote *the Iliad* about 700–800 b.c. It tells of the Greek heroes, particularly Achilles, as they fought against Troy to reclaim Helen, wife of Menelaus, king of Sparta. The story of the fall of Troy and of the horse left behind by the Greeks appears in the *Aeneid*, written by the Roman poet Virgil between 42 and 35 b.c. Ron & Justine Fontes have based their retelling on these sources and on *The War at Troy*, written by greek poet Quintus of Smyrna around a.d. 375.

STORY BY JUSTINE & RON FONTES

**PENCILS BY GORDON PURCELL
INKS BY BARBARA SCHULZ**

COLORING BY HI-FI DESIGN

LETTERING BY BILL HAUSER

Graphic Universe ™
An imprint of Lerner Publishing Group
241 First Avenue North
Minneapolis, MN 55401 U.S.A.

Website address: www.lernerbooks.com

Library of Congress Cataloging-in-Publication Data

Fontes, Justine.
   The Trojan horse: the fall of Troy / by Justine & Ron Fontes; adapted from Virgil's Aeneid and The war at troy by Quintus of Smyrna; illustrations by Gordon Purcell.
      p.   cm. — (Graphic myths and legends)
   Includes bibliographical references and index.
   ISBN-13: 978-0-8225-3085-5 (lib. bdg. : alk. paper)
   ISBN-10: 0-8225-3085-6 (lib. bdg. : alk. paper)
      1. Trojan War—Comic books, strips, etc.
   2. Graphic novels. I. Fontes, Justine. II. Purcell, Gordon. III. Virgil Aeneis. IV. Quintus, Smyrnaeus, 4th cent. Posthomerica. V. Title. VI. Series: Graphic Myths and Legends (Minneapolis, Minn.)
   BL793.T7F66 2007
   741.5'673—dc22   2005023776

Manufactured in the United States of America
1 2 3 4 5 6 - JR - 12 11 10 09 08 07

TABLE OF CONTENTS

A ROTTEN APPLE

HISTORY IS FULL OF WARS. BUT ONE WAR WILL NEVER BE FORGOTTEN. OVER THREE THOUSAND YEARS AGO, THE GREEKS GATHERED THE *GREATEST* ARMY THE WORLD HAD EVER SEEN. ONE THOUSAND SHIPS SAILED TO TAKE THE MIGHTY CITY OF TROY. FOR TEN YEARS, THE BEST WARRIORS WAGED FIERCE BATTLE. BUT TROY'S TALL WALLS STILL STOOD. WHY WERE THEY FIGHTING? THE *TROUBLE STARTED WITH A WEDDING!*

FOR THE FAIREST

ONE GREEK KING MADE A *BIG* MISTAKE. HE INVITED ALL THE GODS AND GODDESSES TO HIS WEDDING, *EXCEPT* ERIS, THE GODDESS OF QUARRELS AND STRIFE. SUDDENLY, AT THE HEIGHT OF THE FEASTING AND FUN, *ERIS APPEARED!*

HERE IS A WEDDING PRESENT FOR YOU!

HA! THIS SHOULD MAKE A BEAUTIFUL BRAWL!

LOOK, A GOLDEN APPLE!

IT'S FOR *ME.* YOU SEE? IT SAYS IT'S FOR THE *FAIREST.*

WHO SAYS YOU ARE THE *FAIREST*? AM I NOT THE QUEEN OF THE GODS?

Uh-oh! THIS MEANS *TROUBLE!*

WHO DO *YOU* THINK IS THE PRETTIEST?

I WOULDN'T *DARE* TO SAY!

IF YOU ASK *ME,* IT'S ATHENA.

WHO ASKED YOU?

PARIS WAS NOT *JUST* A SHEPHERD. HE WAS ALSO A *PRINCE*, THE SON OF KING PRIAM AND QUEEN HECUBA OF TROY.

BUT WHEN PARIS WAS BORN, A WISE MAN *WARNED* THE ROYAL COUPLE ABOUT THE BOY'S FUTURE.

PRINCE PARIS WILL CAUSE YOUR KINGDOM'S DOWNFALL!

MY ADVICE IS TO *KILL* HIM NOW.

OH NO!

WHAT IF THE SAGE IS *WRONG*? OUR BEAUTIFUL BABY!

WHAT IF HE IS *RIGHT*? WE'D BETTER DO SOMETHING.

WE'LL SEND PARIS FAR FROM THE CITY. WHAT *HARM* CAN HE DO IN A MEADOW, TENDING SHEEP?

19

THE TERRIFIED CROWD PARTED AS THE CREATURES SPED TOWARD LAOCOÖN AND HIS SONS. THEIR *FORKED TONGUES* FLICKED, AND THEIR *RED EYES* FLASHED.

WITH A HORRIBLE HISSING, THE SERPENTS SANK THEIR FANGS INTO THE BOYS AND CAPTURED THEM IN THEIR CRUSHING COILS.

HELP! DADDY!

HELP!

LAOCOÖN TRIED TO HELP BUT WAS SOON OVERPOWERED BY THE HIDEOUS CREATURES.

LET THEM GO, YOU FIENDS!

MY FAMILY! WON'T SOMEONE SAVE *MY FAMILY*?

HERA, HAVE MERCY!

IT'S THE WILL OF THE GODS FOR DEFILING THIS OFFERING!

SO THE PRIEST AND HIS SONS SANK BENEATH THE WAVES.

POSEIDON MUST HAVE SENT THE SERPENTS!

25

THE TROJANS DECIDED THE DEATH OF LAOCOON MUST BE A SIGN THAT ATHENA WAS ANGRY AT THE PRIEST FOR SPEARING HER STATUE. THEY QUICKLY WIDENED THE CITY GATES AND PUT THE HORSE ON ROLLERS. THE SURVIVING MEN OF TROY GLADLY LENT THEIR STRENGTH TO PUSH IT THROUGH THE WIDENED GATES INTO THE MAIN SQUARE OF THE CITY.

WE'LL TAKE IT TO ATHENA'S TEMPLE!

EXHAUSTED WITH JOY, FOOD, AND WINE, THE TROJANS SOON SLEPT SOUNDLY. INSTEAD OF SHARPLY STEPPING SENTRIES AND THE QUIET CLINK OF SHOULDERED SWORDS, THE NIGHT WAS FILLED WITH SNORES.

SLEEP *DEEP,* MY TRUSTING ENEMIES!

DURING THE DARKEST HOUR OF THE NIGHT, SINON QUIETLY CLIMBED A TALL TOWER.

ON THE NEARBY ISLAND OF TENEDOS, A GREEK SENTRY SAW THE SIGNAL'S *FIERY FLASH* AGAINST THE BLACK SKY.

PRAISE ATHENA! KING AGAMEMNON, *THE SIGNAL!*

THIS SIGNAL CAN BE SEEN *FOR MILES* AT SEA.

STRONG ARMS LIFTED ANCHORS, UNFURLED SAILS, AND SLAPPED OARS INTO THE WATER. IN *MINUTES*, THE MIGHTY GREEK FLEET WAS ON ITS WAY BACK TO TROY.

FASTER, MEN! TO TROY—*AND VICTORY!*

MEANWHILE, SINON SNEAKED PAST SLEEPING TROJANS TO THE WOODEN HORSE.

HE OPENED A HATCH HIDDEN IN THE BEAST'S LEG. THE SMELL OF MANY MEN CONFINED IN CLOSE QUARTERS GREETED HIM.

IT'S *TIME!*

I MUST FIND PRIAM! THE KING MUST DIE!

42

GLOSSARY AND PRONUNCIATION GUIDE

ACHILLES (uh-*kil*-eez): son of Peleus and Thetis; prince of Phthia and Greek hero

AGAMEMNON (a-ga-*mem*-non): king of Mycenae; high king of the Achaeans

AJAX (*ay*-jax): Greek hero

APHRODITE (a-fro-*dye*-tee): goddess of love

APOLLO (uh-*pol*-oh): god of prophesy, music, and healing

ARES (*air*-eez): the god of war

ATHENA (uh-*thee*-nuh): goddess of wisdom

CASSANDRA (kuh-*san*-druh): daughter of King Priam and Queen Hecuba

ERIS (*ee*-ris): the goddess of discord

HADES (*hay*-deez): god of the dead

HECUBA (*hek*-yoo-buh): wife of King Priam

HELEN (*hell*-en): wife of King Menelaus

HERA (*hehr*-ruh): queen of the gods; goddess of the hearth

LAOCOÖN (lay-*uh*-koh-uhn): priest of Poseidon. He was killed by serpents after warning Troy to destroy the Trojan horse.

MENELAUS (meh-neh-*lay*-uhs): king; brother of Agamemnon

NEOPTOLEMUS (nee-op-*to*-leh-muhs): son of Achilles

ODYSSEUS (o-*dis*-see-uhs): king of Ithaca

PALAMEDES (pa-luh-*mee*-deez): prince of Nauplia; cousin of Agamemnon

PARIS (*pa*-ris): son of King Priam and Queen Hecuba

PENELOPE (pe-*nel*-oh-pee): wife of Odysseus

POSEIDON (po-*seye*-duhn): god of the ocean and earthquakes

PRIAM (*preye*-am): king of Troy

SINON (*si*-non): Greek spy who deceived Troy into bringing the Trojan horse into the city

ZEUS (*zyoos*): king of the gods; god of thunder and the sky

ink from pages 6-7

FURTHER READING AND WEBSITES

d'Aulaire, Ingri, and Edgar Parin d'Aulaire. *Book of Greek Myths*. New York: Dell Publishing, 1992.

Evslin, Bernard. *The Trojan War*. New York: Scholastic Book Services, 1971.

Fleischman, Paul. *Dateline, Troy*. Cambridge, MA: Candlewick Press, 1996.

Greek Myths—History for Kids
http://www.historyforkids.org/learn/greeks/religion/greekrelig.htm
This site provides information about Greek gods, heroes, and myths, as well as information about the Trojan War. It also includes links to related characters, websites, and books located in other websites.

Green, Roger Lancelyn. *The Tale of Troy: Retold from the Ancient Authors*. Baltimore: Puffin Books, 1958.

Hovey, Kate. *Voices of the Trojan War*. New York: Margaret K. McElderry Books, 2004.

McLaren, Clemence. *Inside the Walls of Troy: A Novel of the Women Who Lived the Trojan War*. New York: Atheneum, 1996.

Mythweb
http://www.mythweb.com/gods/index.html
This is an informative site about gods, heroes, and others. It also includes a link to the website's *Encyclopedia of Greek Mythology*.

Sutcliffe, Rosemary. *Black Ships Before Troy: The Story of the Iliad*. New York: Delacorte Press, 1993.

CREATING *THE TROJAN HORSE*

Ancient legends of a war between the Greek city states and Troy that may have taken place around 1200 B.C. were gathered into great epic poems by writers of later times. The Greek poet Homer wrote *The Iliad* about 700–800 B.C. It tells of the Greek heroes, particularly Achilles, as they fought against Troy to reclaim Helen, wife of Menelaus, king of Sparta. The story of the fall of Troy and of the horse left behind by the Greeks appears in the *Aeneid*, written by the Roman poet Virgil between 42 and 35 B.C. Ron & Justine Fontes have based their retelling on these sources and on *The War at Troy*, written by the Greek poet Quintus of Smyrna around A.D. 375.

INDEX

ABOUT THE AUTHORS AND ARTIST

RON & JUSTINE FONTES met at a publishing house in New York City. Ron worked for the comic book department, and Justine was an editorial assistant in children's books. Together they have written nearly 500 children's books, in every format from board books to historical novels.

From their home in Maine, the Fonteses publish *critter news*, a strictly-for-fun newsletter. They also launched Sonic Comics with their first graphic novel, *Tales of a Terminal Diner*, a unique anthology with continuing characters. Other published projects include *The Trojan Horse: The Fall of Troy* and *The Wooden Sword*. Life-long library lovers, the Fonteses long to write 1,1001 books before retiring.

GORDON PURCELL has had an extensive comic career, with credits including five different crews of StarTrek, The X-Files, Silver Sable, Superman, JLA, Robin, Aquaman, Flash, Wonder Man, Avengers, Lost in Space, Soulsearchers, and Xena. He's currently drawing issues of Flare for Heroic, Justice League Unlimited for DC, as well as biography comics. He lives in the frozen tundra of Minnesota with wife, Debra, and son, Jack.